Pocket Devotions for Lent

Dear Tom + Mary,

40 Days
and 40 Nights

Praying through ~~Lent~~
Cancer !!

One day at a time by ~~God's~~
grace!! You are in the
prayers and love of
so very many of us !!
Love-Prayers,
Pastor Nancy
May 8, 2012

Gail Ramshaw

Augsburg Fortress

MINNEAPOLIS

FORTY DAYS AND FORTY NIGHTS
Praying through Lent

ISBN-13: 978-0-8006-2344-9
ISBN-10: 0-8006-2344-4

Cover art: *Empty Yourself Full, No. 2,* © 2002 Daniel Nevins. All rights reserved. Used by permission. www.danielnevins.com
Cover design: Laurie Ingram
Editors: Robert Buckley Farlee, Michelle L. N. Cook

Manufactured in the U.S.A.

13 12 11 10 09 08 07 06   1 2 3 4 5 6 7 8 9 10

Ash Wednesday: Lent is . . .
Day 1	ashes
Day 2	forty
Day 3	the poor
Day 4	treasure

Lent 1: facing evil
Day 5	food
Day 6	mountain
Day 7	garden
Day 8	wind
Day 9	journey
Day 10	the name of God

Lent 2: beginning again in baptism
Day 11	mother
Day 12	heaven
Day 13	cross
Day 14	prophet
Day 15	sacrifice
Day 16	city

Lent 3: gathering in community
Day 17	water
Day 18	outsider
Day 19	temple
Day 20	wisdom
Day 21	harvest
Day 22	covenant

Lent 4: receiving mercy
Day 23	light
Day 24	shepherd
Day 25	tree
Day 26	family
Day 27	creation
Day 28	judge

Lent 5: awaiting God's promises
Day 29	resurrection
Day 30	clothing
Day 31	Israel
Day 32	spirit
Day 33	fish
Day 34	marriage

Passion Sunday: encountering Christ
Day 35	body
Day 36	day of the LORD
Day 37	kingdom
Day 38	servant
Day 39	emanation of the divine
Day 40	battle

INTRODUCTION

FOR YOUR KEEPING OF LENT, this prayer guide is both traditional and contemporary. Over the centuries, Christians have kept Lent by praying more than usual. To assist you in this traditional Lenten practice, *Forty Days and Forty Nights* offers a meditation, a prayer, a Bible reading, and a hymn from *Evangelical Lutheran Worship* for each day's use. (Many of these hymns, or similar ones, can also be found in other resources.)

This book is also contemporary because it connects daily Lenten prayer to our church's Sunday Bible readings. Each Sunday over a three-year pattern, countless Christians around the world read the same scripture selections, and this prayer guide carries these three readings into the days of the week. Following the emphases of our Sunday Bible selections, *Forty Days and Forty Nights* keeps Lent as a time to return to the waters of baptism, join with other Christians in a renewal of our faith, meditate on the meaning of the death of Christ, and enter more fully into the life of the triune God.

Each day's prayer is inspired by an image from one of the Sunday readings. This image becomes the seed of the meditation, like the main ingredient of the meal. (Further thoughts about these forty images can be found in the book *Treasures Old and New*, also from Augsburg Fortress.)

How do images work? An example is the artwork on the cover of this book. With her arms upraised in the ancient posture of prayer, a woman stands in a boat that has a fruitful tree for a sail. Let this be an image of our Lent. We are this woman, sailing across the waters of baptism in the ship of the church. (Think of the "nave" of your church, and recall the word "navy.") We gather around the cross; yet as people of Easter we discover that the mast of our ship is the tree of life itself.

ASH WEDNESDAY,
DAY ONE
Ashes

Is such the fast that I choose, a day to humble
oneself, . . . and to lie in sackcloth and ashes?
Isaiah 58:5, alternate first reading for Ash Wednesday

A WOMAN TO REMEMBER on Ash Day is Tamar. The story
goes that Tamar, one of King David's daughters, was raped by
Ammon, her half-brother. According to ancient Israelite law, the
rapist had to marry the woman he had violated, but of course
Ammon could not marry his half-sister. In her time and place,
this violence meant the end of her world, and in her unbearable
shame, she tore her clothes and poured ashes on her head. The
story says that two years later, her brother Absolom murdered
Ammon, but about Tamar we hear no more. She might as well
be dead.

In the literature of the Old Testament, ashes signify not only
shame, but also penitence. We read that prophet Daniel, bereft
by the political oppression that Israel was suffering, enacted what
many Hebrew poems suggested: with fasting, sackcloth, and ashes,
he prayed to God for forgiveness. He was sure that the people's
devastation had been brought about by their own sins. So Daniel
sat in ashes and begged God for mercy.

Here are two pictures for Ash Wednesday: a woman grieving
the end of a worthy life and a man confessing the sins of a
nation. At the start of Lent, with Tamar we acknowledge that
our plans for a happy life, indeed our life itself, will come to an
end, and with Daniel we ask God to what degree our misery
is our own fault. The ancient tale of the serpent in the garden
suggests that the two are intertwined. According to the story in
Genesis 3, it was because of the disobedience of Adam and Eve
that every soil-man, every bone-woman, each humus-human,
turns back to soil. We hear the echo of this story over and over

in the Ash Wednesday liturgy: "Remember that you are dust, and to dust you shall return." This is the day when Christians mark themselves with the ashes of these two inescapable truths: we sin daily, and we will die.

The ash day of Lent is some ninety days before the fire day of Pentecost. Our ashes will be washed off in the font and replaced with tongues of fire. This is an odd reversal, since we know that fire produces ashes, not ashes fire. Yet the Christian faith proclaims a truth quite different from the facts of nature. Although we and all we love will end in ash, we place our confidence not in nature but in divine grace. From death will come life; from ashes will arise the fire of the Spirit of God.

Look upon the ashes of our pain, O grieving God.
Wash away the ashes of our regret, O sorrowing
Holy One. Burn them away with the fire of your
Spirit. May it be so: Amen.

Reading: 1 Samuel 2:1-10

Hymn: *ELW* 451, "We Are Baptized in Christ Jesus," stanzas 1-2

THURSDAY AFTER ASH WEDNESDAY, DAY TWO
Forty

I will send rain on the earth for forty days and forty nights.
Genesis 7:4

POPE GREGORY THE GREAT said that the church keeps Lent for forty days because we multiply the ten commandments by the four gospels. Historians suggest, instead, that since ancient Israel lived by the lunar calendar, the usual period of reckoning was twenty-eight days. Thus "forty days" designated an extraordinary span of time, a time that stood out as longer than the normal. The Bible says that for forty days the rain fell on Noah's ark, Moses fasted on Mount Sinai, the spies scouted out Canaan, Israel's armies were taunted by Goliath, Elijah walked on the strength of the angel's food to the mountain of God, Ezekiel lay on his right side, the inhabitants of Nineveh repented, Jesus wandered in the wilderness, and he appeared after the resurrection. Although a woman was unclean for eighty days after the birth of a daughter, the time was forty days after the birth of a son. Forty days was the time between the start and the finish, the period in which to prepare for the fruition.

Christians continue this forty-day pattern. By the fourth century, the church allotted forty days as the time for preparation of adult baptisms at the great Vigil of Easter and for the penance of notorious sinners. Several centuries later, with both Easter baptisms and public penances becoming rare, Lent came to focus on the passion of Christ and on personal rituals of penitence. For many people Lent is a time to meditate on the sufferings of Jesus and to suffer a tiny bit by, oh, perhaps, giving up chocolate. (By the way, to compute the forty days, we don't count the six Sundays, since Sunday is always a celebration of the resurrection; so eating chocolate on Sundays seems okay.)

Genesis says that at Noah's flood the windows of the sky opened, and the waters above the sky poured down, and the waters underground gushed up. In other words, the earth was returned to its primeval watery chaos. The ark landed onto a new creation, God's life having reemerged from earth's death. Forty rainy days, and the earth is born anew.

Perhaps for you Lent means more personal prayer, more service projects, more thank-you notes, a midweek Bible study, fewer quarrels, less bad-mouthing, minimal meals, no movies. According to our Sunday readings, Lent is the time for the entire community to board ship and sail through the waters of baptism to Easter. However you make Lent a time other than the ordinary, you know that you keep Lent with millions of believers around the world. Together we are crammed into the ark, floating together on God's mercy, trusting the wood of Christ's ship for our safety, waiting to glimpse the arrival of the dove.

> *O God, our beginning and our end, you provide us*
> *a time to feast and a time to fast, a time to embark*
> *and a time to return home. Give us companions for*
> *our journey as we navigate toward you. May it be so:*
> *Amen.*

Reading: Ecclesiastes 3:1-8

Hymn: *ELW* 319, "O Lord, throughout These Forty Days," stanzas 1, 4

FRIDAY AFTER ASH WEDNESDAY, DAY THREE
The poor

Paul wrote, "They asked only one thing, that we remember the poor, which was actually what I was eager to do."
Galatians 2:10

IN HER OLD AGE, Margot Fontaine, one of the premier ballerinas of the twentieth century, described the grueling discipline of her career as a gift. She always knew what to do every morning after breakfast: go to the barre and begin exercising. The dancer's discipline brought order to her days, and this order cleared the pathway for beauty. But many college students say that if you don't like grandma's gift, you should not send a thank-you note. They judge the formal disciplines of gratitude as hypocrisy; it's better to honor your personal feelings than to lie to your grandmother. So: is discipline wholesome or hurtful? Does discipline nurture the self, or does it squash the self?

The gospel from Matthew 6 that has been read on Ash Wednesday for centuries suggests what the medieval church called "the Lenten disciplines": we are to give alms, pray, and fast—that is, contribute to the needs of the poor, pray often and deeply, and resist all forms of self-indulgence. Today, a Friday, the day always marked for Christians by Christ's crucifixion, we join Paul in remembering the poor. Such an exercise will take the whole of Lent's forty days, for there are so many of the poor lying on our doorstep, attended only by stray dogs: victims of torture, of war, of natural disasters, of lousy education, more and more victims; migrant workers; the unemployed; peasants in developing countries; refugees; orphans in sub-Saharan Africa; many Native Americans; girls sold into prostitution; and we have not yet listed those who are poor in spirit, those who suffer abuse or prejudice or depression or abandonment. It takes a long time to remember the poor.

For Christians, remembering the poor is nothing other than seeing clearly one's own left or right hand. We are the body of Christ, with no great chasm fixed between rich and poor, no railroad tracks dividing the community. God is with the poor, sings Mary to Elizabeth. God is on their side. So Lent urges us to remember them, join with them, contribute toward their needs, visit them, serve them food, find ways that the nation might enact more justice on their behalf, pray for them. Such a list.

You surprise us, O God, hanging naked on the cross.
We worship you, O Lord, who had nowhere to lay
your head. Hold in our minds and hearts everyone
who likewise is poor. May it be so: Amen.

Reading: Luke 16:19-31

Hymn: *ELW* 479, "We Come to the Hungry Feast"

SATURDAY AFTER ASH WEDNESDAY, DAY FOUR
Treasure

Where your treasure is, there your heart will be also.
Matthew 6:21, gospel for Ash Wednesday

LENT IS A TREASURE. Mercifully, for Christians, life is not one damn day after another. Gems appear. One day in seven is a resurrection celebration. In the cold time of the year, the warmth of the sun is reborn in a manger. Each year Easter comes to renew the year. And the forty days of Lent point us toward the poor, urge us to prayer, and help us restrain our appetites. Lent shimmers its deep purple around us.

Our neighbors are a treasure. Mercifully, each of us does not live isolated, a castaway on an island, cracking open coconuts, talking to lizards. When Quakers in the nineteenth century tried to reform criminals by locking them in solitary confinement with a Bible, many of them went psychotic. We are communal creatures, fed, clothed, embraced, employed, accompanied by one another our life long. The sisters of Mother Teresa of Calcutta see as their mission to hold the dying, for even if one cannot live in someone's arms, at least one can die in a warm embrace. When St. Lawrence was ordered by the police to hand over to the state the treasures of the church, he said, Okay, I'll bring them to you in three days—at which time he presented to the officers the church's poor and sick, saying, "These are the treasures of the church."

Baptism is a treasure. Mercifully, God provides us water, rain, rivers, oceans, geysers. Several gallons in a font renew us once and for all. The drops of water we place on our forehead each time we pass the font glisten like gems right where our ashes had been.

Because these treasures come hidden in clay jars, we might not recognize that they are gold and silver, a ruby here, a sapphire there. But even these treasures are only a down payment on the treasure that is God. They are only a pearl or two toward the necklace that is divine grace. If God is our treasure, we are rich. We can never be totally alone because we meet one another there in God.

Yet Julian of Norwich, the medieval mystic famous for calling God our mother, claimed that we are the crown that God wears. Julian reversed the image: we are God's treasure. If she was right, we'd best wash the muck off so that we can shine.

> *Make us skilled appraisers, O precious Holy One,*
> *so that we discard the trash and treasure your gifts,*
> *valuing each gem that you place in our path. May it*
> *be so: Amen.*

Reading: Matthew 13:44-45

Hymn: *ELW* 775, "Jesus, Priceless Treasure"

FIRST SUNDAY IN LENT
FACING EVIL

A
Genesis 2:15-17; 3:1-7
Romans 5:12-19
Matthew 4:1-11
Think about what forbidden fruits we are tempted to eat.
Give thanks for all of God's free gifts.

B
Genesis 9:8-17
1 Peter 3:18-22
Mark 1:9-15
Think about the evils that God must wash away.
Give thanks for God's Spirit alighting on us.

C
Deuteronomy 26:1-11
Romans 10:8b-13
Luke 4:1-13
Think about the harsh treatments and wilderness wanderings we
suffer through.
Give thanks for angelic protection.

O loving God, to turn away from you is to fall, to turn toward
you is to rise, and to stand before you is to abide forever. Grant
us, dear God, in all our duties your help; in all our uncertainties
your guidance; in all our dangers your protection; and in all our
sorrows your peace; through Jesus Christ our Lord. Amen.
(A prayer of Augustine of Hippo, *ELW* p. 87)

MONDAY OF LENT 1, DAY FIVE
Food

Command these stones to become loaves of bread.
Matthew 4:3, gospel for Lent 1 A

EACH YEAR THE READINGS for the first Sunday of Lent speak of food. In Eden the woman and the man eat the forbidden fruit, thus biting into their own death; yet Canaan flows with milk and honey, providing the people both sustenance and dessert. We hear of plentiful food—the pious Israelites offering their first fruits in gratitude to God—and of extreme fast—Jesus eating nothing for forty days and forty nights.

"Food, food, I must have food! The trees are bare and the ground is frozen and I can't find anything to eat," cried the starving grasshopper in the wintertime, and according to the fable, the colony of ants feeds him. We are that grasshopper, trying to survive on a diet of stones. With our belly bulging with gravel, there is no room for bread, milk, and honey. Our stomachs complain; even if the pebbles are tiny diamonds, they will not keep us alive.

Lent is a time to give up eating stones. In medieval Europe Lent was a time for fasting. Anthropologists suggest that this ritual developed because in late winter, before springtime produced any new crops, the north was running out of food, and it makes sense to turn human necessity into religious benefit. But Christians believed that they were replicating the life of Jesus, who in turn was replicating the experience of the Israelites. We join Elijah on his forty-day hunger hike, heading toward the mountain of God. For forty days, many believers find some way to fast, depriving themselves of at least treats, if not staples. In so doing, Christians practice dying, sharpen their discipline, identify with the poor, and realize our reliance on God. In the words of one of our Lenten prayers, we fast from self-indulgence, if not for our entire baptized life, at least for forty days each year. The hope is that if we are not overstuffed with ourselves, we will have room for others.

Rather than stones, we take in the word of God. We eat of Christ, who is life. Church art often depicted the manna raining down from the sky onto the Israelites as tiny communion hosts, for believers knew the weekly meal to be the food of God. Catherine of Siena, a medieval mystic whose extreme fasting led to her death, called the triune God her food, her table, and her server. God is the sustenance of our life, the weekly table at which we eat, and the one who serves up the meal. We can learn from Catherine not her unbalanced asceticism, but her fervent prayer to God.

Replace our diet of stones with yourself, O God. Feed us and all who hunger, that we may live. Train us to wait tables with your gracious Spirit. May it be so: Amen.

Reading: Psalm 119:97-104, 169-176

Hymn: *ELW* 658, "O Jesus, Joy of Loving Hearts," stanzas 1, 2, 4

TUESDAY OF LENT 1, DAY SIX
Mountain

The devil took [Jesus] to a very high mountain and showed him all the kingdoms of the world and their splendor.
Matthew 4:8, gospel for Lent 1 A

MATTHEW WROTE THAT THE devil brought Jesus to the top of a very high mountain so they could view all the wealth of the world. Perhaps Matthew imagined that there was such a mountain, a vantage point from which to scan a flat earth. Perhaps our television is such a mountain: all of the earth's civilizations are laid out before our eyes, and the commercials tempt us to acquire the splendor of the nations.

During this first week of Lent, we join Jesus and the devil up on that mountain, facing the perpetual temptation to want more, to have more, to conquer the world. The mountain had better be more like a mesa than a peak, for it will be crowded up there, zillions of people enjoying the vista, imagining their loot, computing their catch. We are told that to own the world, we must worship the devil, which, sad to say, we do rather regularly. So it seems the devil is lying, since we have not received all the world's splendor as reward.

Lent sets out before our eyes not only the mountain of temptation, but also the mountain of God. The Bible speaks often of a holy mountain from which God teaches us the difference between good and evil, a place where we see Jesus transfigured into the appearance of a god, a mountain where at the end of time—when finally evil is over—we will join with everyone in a feast marked by harmony and plenty. In one story, Elijah, nearly defeated by the power of King Ahab and Queen Jezebel, walks for forty days and forty nights to reach the mountain of God. There in "a sound of sheer silence"—the Hebrew of the text is odd, the translators debate how to say this in English—Elijah encounters God. We might imagine that God is glad to have Elijah there for a religious retreat, a short break from evil. Yet God sends him back to confront the evil of Ahab's kingdom and share with others the word of the Lord.

Usually we want more than a sound of sheer silence; we were hoping for the most magnificent concert this world has ever heard. Yet it may be that for a time "a still small voice" is all we are given. Together we gather around that word of God, reminding one another that the Spirit speaks in surprising ways, in a timbre quite other than the blaring bellow of the world. We huddle close to listen, so that when I can't quite make out a word, you can tell me what I missed.

Lead us up your mountain, O God, our leader, our guide, and give us companions to lean on, your voice to hear, your splendor to see. May it be so: Amen.

Reading: Isaiah 2:1-5

Hymn: *ELW* 315, "How Good, Lord, to Be Here!" stanzas 1, 4, 5

WEDNESDAY OF LENT 1, DAY SEVEN
Garden

*You may freely eat of every tree of the garden; but of
the tree of the knowledge of good and evil you shall
not eat.*
Genesis 2:16-17, first reading for Lent 1 A

WHERE DOES EVIL COME from? How did evil begin? Who or what
is to blame for the wickedness that we renounce during Lent?

In addressing this age-old religious question, the Bible
presents two different stories. The second story says that evil
arose even before humans were on the scene. Revelation 12
blames the dragon Satan for causing a cosmic rebellion. Evil
persists because this war has not yet reached an armistice.
Although this Darth Vader narrative captures the imagination of
many people, Lent does nothing with it.

Rather, the church has sought more truth in the legend of
the garden. The creation story in Genesis 2–3 says that at the
beginning God planted a garden, in the center of which were
two trees, one that granted immortality and the other that
offered, well, what? Why would God forbid the knowledge of
good and evil? Does the woman get what the serpent promised?
The couple, suddenly grown-up, covers their naked bodies
and cowers in God's presence. They hoped for advancement,
but found themselves in disgrace. Yet the story does not fully
satisfy our search for the origin of evil. Theologians struggled
to explain why God would create a serpent who would speak
temptation, and they found one answer in the later story of the
satanic dragon.

The church uses these stories to teach what many of the
world's religions claim: that evil exists because day after day
humans choose it. Because evil is so deceptive and our judgment
so partial, we do not perceive evil for what it is. We confuse
wheat and weeds. We prune the tree, only to discover that we
have killed it. We want the garden to be only vibrant green,

fragrant flowers and luscious fruitfulness. Yet the pathways we stroll lead to the centerpiece of the garden: the tree of our downfall. We are startled, befuddled.

We know that first-century Palestinians did not bury their dead in gardens. Jews judged tombs to be unclean, and Romans, viewing cemeteries as desecrations, located them outside the city walls. Yet the Gospel of John places Jesus' burial in a garden, and in that garden Mary Magdalene meets the risen Christ, who in some way resembles a gardener. We had thought that a crucifixion yields a rotting body on a trash heap; instead, Christ's cross leads to personal transformation, communal vigor, and resurrection joy. We are startled, transfigured.

O God our gardener, creator of all that is good, point out to us the poisonous plants, the treacherous trees. Water our garden with your lively Spirit. May it be so: Amen.

Reading: Isaiah 58:6-11

Hymn: *ELW* 690, "We Raise Our Hands to You" stanzas 1-3

THURSDAY OF LENT 1, DAY EIGHT
Wind

When I bring clouds over the earth, . . . I will
remember my covenant that is between me and you
and every living creature of all flesh.
Genesis 9:14-15, first reading for Lent 1 B

DURING THIS FIRST WEEK of Lent we look the devil straight in the eye and face the forces of misery in the world. One misery comes with clouds and winds: not the cool breeze of the early evening, when God takes a walk in the garden, but the storm that wrecked Paul's ship near Crete, or the cataclysmic flood of Noah that like an ice age compelled human society to begin all over again. Today we focus on such devastation and off-the-charts death, on typhoons and hurricanes that destroy lives and engender sorrow for unnumbered thousands. If such a wind is not this month ripping the roof off our houses, it is tearing apart the world of some community somewhere.

The cross of Ash Wednesday signifies not only our sinfulness, our selfish stupidities one after another, but also our mortality. We will die. All of us go down to the dust. The winds of nature do not care how long we live, whether our house will be leveled, whether we will thrive until the grandchildren are grown. The wind blows where it will, knocking down everything in its path, including us. Perhaps Jesus will calm the storm, but perhaps not.

Yet in the church, as in the synagogue of old, we help one another believe that the power of storm and tempest is weaker than the strength of God. The wind is not like a deity whose might we try to pacify. In Hebrew, the noun for "wind" is the same word that is used for the "breath" of God and the "spirit" of the Eternal One. Believers foster the hope that what we experience as the force of satanic destruction is less than, or perhaps somehow contained within, the inexplicable vigor of God. We are not tossed back and forth between two warring forces, one good and one evil. There is only one God. The broken mast of our smashed boat is, we pray, none other than the cross of Christ.

When we are toppled by the wind, it is not easy to believe that God is greater than the storm. So it is a gift that we are given one another. Roped together, we might be able to withstand the tempest. By our baptism, we commit ourselves to helping one another stand. When one of us is knocked breathless, down on hands and knees, another is standing there, praying for strength.

> *Merciful God, creator of the universe, when winds wreck our ship, breathe your spirit of hope into your people, that even at the grave we sing your praise. May it be so: Amen.*

Reading: Mark 4:35-41

Hymn: *ELW* 396, "Spirit of Gentleness," stanzas 1, 3, 4

FRIDAY OF LENT 1, DAY NINE
Journey

> *The* LORD *brought us out of Egypt . . . and he brought*
> *us into this place and gave us this land.*
> Deuteronomy 26:8-9, first reading for Lent 1 C

MOST OF US HAVE never embarked on a journey. We take road
trips, and go on hikes, and enjoy vacation travel, maybe splurge
on a cruise, perhaps even join an expedition. But a journey
is a lengthy ordeal, marked by the unexpected, the delightful
or disastrous. In 1742, Henry Melchior Muhlenberg left his
comfortable homeland in Germany and sailed to colonial
Pennsylvania to minister to its Lutheran churches. When the
ship ran out of drinking water, the rats, who also were thirsty,
licked the sweat off the passengers' faces while they slept.
That's a journey. In the 1930s, migrants who had been forced
off their drought-ravaged farms drove out to California in
their jalopies, fueled by the myth of fruit trees ripe for picking,
only to encounter yet more wretched poverty. That's a journey.
The Israelite creed recorded in Deuteronomy 26 speaks of the
beginning of the journey—slavery in Egypt—and of the end
of the journey—arrival in the land of milk and honey. Of the
journey itself, the decades of woeful nomadic life, this creed says
only that God helped them through.

Each year, the first Sunday of Lent tells of Jesus' journey into
the desert. In his forty days in the wilderness, Jesus relived the
history of God's chosen people. The ancient Israelites, having
left Egypt, endured hunger and temptation in the wilderness,
before they could enter the new land of promise. Now too Jesus,
who in one telling also came out from Egypt, wandered through
hunger and temptation in the wilderness. The journey of Jesus,
like that of the people of Israel, is the human odyssey, from the
restriction of the womb, through life's adventures and agonies,
toward a promised fulfillment.

In Lent we join Jesus in his journey from death into the new land of life, traveling together from Ash Wednesday to Easter. Because the church knows that the Lenten journey is arduous, many Christians assemble not only on Sunday but also midweek, helping one another through the forty days in the wilderness. The font is filled with baptismal waters, flowing from the rock of Christ for us, so that during this journey we always have water at our side.

This journey is not like some weekend vacation, carefully planned and pleasantly enjoyed. Rather, this journey is more like the Mexican family willing to risk the desert in order to find work. One American family intended that their visit to Sri Lanka would be a relaxing Christmas vacation. Instead, the 2004 tsunami made of their trip a journey, and their lives will never be the same. Perhaps Lent can be also, not a blip on our annual screen, but the start of a whole new way to arrive at God.

> *Journey with us, O pilgrim God. Be our guide, our water source, our walking stick. Be the home that welcomes us at the end. May it be so: Amen.*

Reading: Exodus 17:1-7

Hymn: *ELW* 326, "Bless Now, O God, the Journey"

SATURDAY OF LENT 1, DAY TEN
The name of God

*Everyone who calls upon the name of the Lord shall
be saved.*
Romans 10:13, second reading for Lent 1 C

ACCORDING TO THE BIBLICAL worldview, one's name signifies
one's self. Abram, Sarai, Jacob, Simon, and Saul all change their
name when their relationship with God changes their life. When
Moses seeks for the strength to appear before Pharaoh, God
calls out from the burning bush the power of the divine name.
When Solomon dedicates the temple, he explains that the edifice
houses not God, but the name of God. According to the Ten
Commandments, misusing the divine name is tantamount to
misusing God.

Yet another example of this idea is found in Exodus 28,
which describes the elaborate vesture worn by the Israelite high
priest. Front and center was the breastpiece with twelve different
gemstones set in gold filigree. Each stone carried the name of
one of the tribes of Israel. "So Aaron shall bear the names of the
sons of Israel in the breastpiece of judgment on his heart when
he goes into the holy place, for a continual remembrance before
the LORD" (verse 29). The names of the tribes symbolized the
tribes themselves: by wearing the gems of their names over his
heart, Aaron carried the tribes on his body when he came before
God in the tabernacle.

Fifteen hundred years later, according to the beloved Irish
legend, a Druid king was conducting the springtime fire ritual.
In opposition to these pagan beliefs, and it being Easter Eve,
Patrick lit the paschal fire—the same paschal fire Christians will
light precisely five weeks from tonight. The king ordered the
arrest of the insubordinate missionary, but Patrick took cover
behind the name of God, singing the incantation we know as
St. Patrick's Breastplate. Patrick bore on his breast the name of
God, and he was kept safe by the power of the Almighty. "I bind

unto myself today the strong name of the Trinity . . . I bind this day to me forever, by power of faith, Christ's incarnation . . . Christ be with me, Christ within me, Christ behind me, Christ before me. . . ." In stanzas we no longer sing, God protects us "against every cruel merciless power that may oppose my body and soul, against incantations of false prophets, against spells of witches and smiths and wizards, against poison, against drowning," against every evil we can imagine.

Lent calls us to consider hunger, temptation, struggle, evil, storm, danger of all kinds. But in baptism, we have been put under the name of God, and we pray that like a breastplate in battle, this strong name of the Trinity will keep us safe. On Ash Wednesday we wore the ashes of our sin and death, but now we wear God's name, safeguarding our days, defending us from the demons that attack us from inside and out.

> *Your holy, immortal, and mighty name, O God, we praise. Save us by your name. Protect us by your truth. May it be so: Amen.*

Reading: John 17:6-19

Hymn: *ELW* 450, "I Bind unto Myself Today"

SECOND SUNDAY IN LENT
BEGINNING AGAIN IN BAPTISM

A
Genesis 12:1-4a
Romans 4:1-5, 13-17
John 3:1-17
Think about what countries we are asked to leave.
Give thanks for a second birth.

B
Genesis 17:1-7, 15-16
Romans 4:13-25
Mark 8:31-38
Think about dreams unfulfilled.
Give thanks for the life that comes to us from God.

C
Genesis 15:1-12, 17-18
Philippians 3:17—4:1
Luke 13:31-35
Think about our demons and diseases.
Give thanks for God's warm embrace.

In you, Father all-mighty, we have our preservation and our
bliss. In you, Christ, we have our restoring and our saving. You
are our mother, brother and savior. In you, our Lord the Holy
Spirit, is marvelous and plenteous grace. You are our clothing;
for love you wrap us and embrace us. You are our maker, our
lover, our keeper. Teach us to believe that by your grace all shall
be well, and all shall be well, and all manner of things shall be
well. Amen.
(A prayer of Julian of Norwich, *ELW* p. 87)

MONDAY OF LENT 2,
DAY ELEVEN
Mother

*No one can enter the kingdom of God without being
born of water and Spirit.*
John 3:5, gospel for Lent 2 A

ONE PSYCHOLOGICAL THEORY PROPOSES that the reason humans
are so stressed is that much of our life's energy remains focused
on recovering from our birth. During the birth process we
infants experienced considerable trauma in leaving our mother's
free food and protective embrace, and the shock of being
disconnected never fully goes away. Perhaps you do not give
this theory much credence, but it is true that nature sets up the
ordeal of birth with the intent that only the strongest survive.
Life is not easy, and so, appropriately, neither is birth, since
nature wants only the hardiest to live.

Perhaps we do spend our lives searching for the comfort and
care of the womb. Perhaps such a hope for continuous support
is at the root of our myth of the mother. We experience this
myth on Mother's Day, when we imagine every mother as a
gracious goddess, freely giving life, willingly nurturing it, and
happily sending it forth. In fairy tales, it is not the mother, but
the stepmother who is a deplorable wretch, more ready to kill
than to cherish.

Lent tells us that our natural birth, whether it was painful
or joyous, is not enough. Back then, at our first birth, we were
born to ourselves, separated from the mother, released into
the world as yet another animal hoping to survive and thrive.
In baptism we are born from above. One's body is no longer
bounded by one's thin skin. Contained within the body of
Christ, we are one with all those who are born once again in the
water of God's grace. My spirit is not only the breath going in
and out of my lungs, but is God's breath, shared with everyone

else who is birthed in baptism. When one of us is weak, the strength of God in the community is there for comfort and strength.

Nicodemus doesn't get it. We sympathize with him, for this gospel is a counter-cultural worldview. In Lent we hear the good news that in the font is our second birth; the church is like a womb, God is like the truest mother who nurtures the whole creation, carries us through life and death, gives us sisters and brothers by the millions, and holds our body safe within the resurrected body of Christ.

> *Enclose us, nurture us, protect us, mother us, O*
> *God. Give us the breath of your Spirit, and connect*
> *us with all our siblings. May it be so: Amen.*

Reading: 1 John 4:16b—5:4

Hymn: *ELW* 735, "Mothering God, You Gave Me Birth"

TUESDAY OF LENT 2, DAY TWELVE
Heaven

No one has ascended into heaven except the one who
descended from heaven, the Son of Man.
John 3:13, gospel for Lent 2 A

THE YOUNG COUPLE PHONES friends with the happy news that
their child is now standing up alone in the crib. Elsewhere, a
son is not growing tall, so a well-meaning neighbor suggests
growth hormones. Our bank balance, our semester grades, the
selling price of our house, up, up, we want at least these to go
up. Cities vie for the tallest skyscrapers, wealthy adventurers
spend hundreds of thousands to climb the earth's highest
mountains. Up seems to be better. Anthropologists speculate
that essential to human evolution was the day that our ancient
ancestors stood upright, and thus they could see farther across
the savannah, to spot both food and predators.

It is common for religion to speak in this same way, as if
what is good is up. The sun and rain, without which we have
no life, these are up. Religions often say that the gods live up
above the sky, and so worshipers raise their arms in prayer, as
if they are reaching for the bounty from above. Moses goes up
to the top of the mountain to commune with the LORD, and
when Elijah leaves this life, he ascends into the sky in a flying
chariot of fire. People speak as if the dead are up in heaven. In
John's Gospel, Jesus tells Nicodemus and us that he has come
down from above to be a human, to join us in looking upward
to God.

Science tells us that there is no "up." In the natural universe,
all directions are all around. To be Christians, we need not
pretend to be ancient peoples thinking that God is actually up
and away above the clouds, and our religious life is the arduous
climb up, up, to reach the distant deity. Rather, Christians say
that "Jesus came down from above" as a way to articulate the
mystery that in Christ, everything we seek comes to us. We

climb a tree to glimpse God, but Christ calls us down for supper. All the heights of human hope are here in Christ. The body of Christ is with us when we gather each week—not above us, but all around.

Yet the imagery of "up" is useful. "Down" is sleep, death, passivity, helplessness. Lent is growing up, from our new birth in baptism, standing tall with all the baptized to embody justice, supporting our neighbor in hope. Lent is standing up in our crib.

> *Exalted are you, God above all. Be with us down here, heaven-high rider of the clouds. Raise us to stand with those in need. May it be so: Amen.*

Reading: Luke 19:1-10

Hymn: *ELW* 510, "Word of God, Come Down on Earth"

WEDNESDAY OF LENT 2, DAY THIRTEEN
Cross

If any want to become my followers, let them deny themselves and take up their cross and follow me.
Mark 8:34, gospel for Lent 2 B

MANY RELIGIONS HAVE WHAT scholars call an "axis mundi," a sacred place that functions as the symbolic center of the world. For Muslims, the Kaaba in Mecca is such a world-center, the holiest place on earth, the spot where the faithful are most completely connected with God. All devout Muslims hope that at least once they can travel to Mecca to experience its transformative power. For some tribal religions, the "axis mundi" is a great central pole. Tradition says the gods came down to earth on this pole, or that the spirits ascend to the heavens on this pole, or that this pole marks the spot where creation began. For the Lakota people of the American Midwest, a cottonwood tree pole centers the midsummer sun dance. When the people gather around the sacred tree, they re-establish their ties with all of creation and access divine power.

For Christians, no geographical location is the holiest place on earth. Our "axis mundi" is the cross, a pole that connects human need with divine power, the hub around which we gather to acknowledge death and receive God's mercy.

We are accustomed to seeing pictures of Jesus carrying his entire cross. However, when the Roman empire executed by crucifixion, upright stakes were permanently set into the ground, like telephone poles, and onto this pole was hoisted the victim, who carried only the crosspiece to the site of execution. Thus Roman law had made of the pole a place of death, rather than a place of life. But Christians claim that, in a double turnaround, what seems to be the death of a man results in life for the world. If the vertical pole is our connection with God, then the horizontal crosspiece, the wood that Jesus carried, links us to one another. The arms of Christ extend out, embracing us all, and we crowd next to each other, holding on to the crosspiece for dear life.

Our faith begins at the cross. The cross is formed by both the upright and the crosspiece, our life marked by God and with the neighbor. Neither is whole without the other. Over and over, thousands of times, we trace the cross on our body. Rather than traveling for miles to find the center of the earth, we carry it on our forehead everywhere we go. The cross is with us always, mystically shining forth from our face.

> *Connect us, living God, to your mercy and might. Attach us, divine Spirit, to one another. Make of us a cross, centered in Christ. May it be so: Amen.*

Reading: 1 Corinthians 1:18-25

Hymn: *ELW* 338, "Beneath the Cross of Jesus"

THURSDAY OF LENT 2,
DAY FOURTEEN
Prophet

[Jesus] said to them,   "Listen, I am casting out
demons and performing cures today and tomorrow,
and on the third day I finish my work."
Luke 13:32, gospel for Lent 2 C

A PROPHET IS SOMEONE who tells the truth about the present situation. Usually the prophet also alludes to what is coming, for part of truth-telling is the honesty to admit that the present inevitably leads toward a certain future. The prophet urges us to stop kidding ourselves: today's problem will not miraculously get itself solved so that we can enjoy a pleasant tomorrow. Sin in the present leads to sorrow in the future: that's the truth, says the prophet.

In Lent we attend to the prophets of ancient and contemporary times. They yell out our present situation: we are not gods, although we like to imagine that we are; this very minute we are on our way to the grave; meanwhile we sin daily, harming ourselves, pushing aside people who stand in our path, walking quickly past those who appeal for our help. Demons are everywhere, sickness impairs those we love. It's not a pretty picture, says the prophet.

The one whom Christians call Christ was a prophet. His ministry began by calling us to recognize the truth of our existence. He told the truth so fully that we call him the very Word of truth. Yet his word surprises us, for he promises a future transformed by divine grace. On the third day, he says, he will finish what we thought was our endless task. He himself will slay the devils and fight disease. All that we dread will lead, not to death, but to God.

On the great Three Days of Easter we will rehearse the demise of the demons and the celebration of cures. Yet we are surrounded by lots of contrary evidence: it doesn't seem as if at the conclusion of these forty days and forty nights, all will be well. So we meet regularly to encourage one another to accept this prophecy of grace. We pray together that on the third day, God will finish all this messy work.

Martin Luther spoke of beginning each day in our baptism. Starting anew, we are not driven by our demons and diseases, but rather we are drawn by the Spirit into God's future. Thanks to this faith, even the harsh words of the prophet come as a gift, for truth finally is preferred over lies and evasion and folly. We stand together in this Word and await the third day.

> *Send our demons away, God of power and might.*
> *Bring cures for our diseases, Lord Christ, prophet of*
> *truth. Give us your Spirit of promise. May it be so:*
> *Amen.*

Reading: 2 Corinthians 1:3-22

Hymn: *ELW* 736, "God the Sculptor of the Mountains," stanza 4

FRIDAY OF LENT 2, DAY FIFTEEN
Sacrifice

*[The LORD] said to [Abram,] "Bring me a heifer
three years old, a female goat three years old, a ram
three years old, a turtle-dove, and a young pigeon."
[Abram] brought him all these and cut them in two.*
Genesis 15:9-10, first reading for Lent 2 C

GENESIS 15 RECORDS ONE of the countless animal sacrifices,
detailed in Exodus and Leviticus, with which the ancient
Israelites worshiped God. The Bible says that even the first
human children, Cain and Abel, offered crops and livestock in
their worship, and that in thanksgiving for God's protection
during the flood, Noah made a sacrifice of "every clean animal
and every clean bird"—quite an immense pile of animal
carcasses.

Offering sacrifices to the deity is one way that Israelite
religion resembled many other religions. For tens of thousands
of years, humans have burned up their animals, their produce,
even their firstborn children, believing that the gods and god-
desses would be pleased with these precious gifts and would
bless the worshipers. If we give the goddess our first child, surely
she will give us nine more! Historians wonder how this idea
got started. One theory is that humans are prone to violence,
and killing something for the gods is better than killing each
other for revenge. A second theory is that humans, watching
childbirth, assume that there is no life without blood and pain.
Perhaps sacrifices arose out of the communal wisdom that in
order to get, you first must give.

Early Christians, contemplating the meaning of Jesus'
execution, also used the language of sacrifice. Christ is the Lamb
of God, slain for us, whose flowing blood drains out divine life
for the world. The New Testament proclaims that Jesus' death is
the only sacrifice needed: we are no longer required to offer this
or that sacrifice. Yet the human impulse to offer something to

God remains. Many churches, when approving the budget, call for "sacrificial giving," and many Christians speak of Lent as a time to sacrifice for others. Less life for you means more life for others.

But some Christians give, give, give so much that there is nearly nothing of themselves left. Perhaps for these believers Lent can be a time to praise God for the sacrifice of Christ, whose life brings an end to sacrifices. God does not ask for our blood-letting, our veins opened to prove our devotion. God wants us to live.

Which are you, not enough sacrifice, or too much? Both groups of Christians have been given the Spirit of Christ in baptism. The Spirit enables us to live for others while assuring us that Christ has already given his life for us.

Burn us up in love for others, O fiery God. Save us from torching ourselves, O loving Savior. By your Lamb, offer us both these gifts. May it be so: Amen.

Reading: Hebrews 10:11-22

Hymn: *ELW* 336, "Lamb of God (Your Only Son)"

SATURDAY OF LENT 2,
DAY SIXTEEN
City

*Jerusalem, Jerusalem, the city that kills the prophets
and stones those who are sent to it!*
Luke 13:34, gospel for Lent 2 C

THROUGHOUT THE BIBLE WE hear about wicked cities. Genesis
4:17 says that the first city was built by the murderer Cain.
Babel, Sodom and Gomorrah, Babylon, Nineveh, Susa, Rome:
from the point of view of the peasants, the big city is the home
of alien peoples, a center of immorality, and a stronghold
of the oppressor. In Luke 13, even Jerusalem is cast as evil,
resisting the word of God. Lots of Christian hymns continue
this tradition, praising nature as beautiful, but citing the evils of
urban life.

Yet the Bible also praises the city. Stunning poems in the Old
Testament cite Jerusalem as the center of God's presence on
earth. Although the human story begins in a garden, Revelation
describes the final home of God's people as a magnificent city.
Its city walls protect the inhabitants from enemies; its twelve
gates indicate great crowds and open exchange; the foundations
are precious gemstones, displaying fabulous wealth; dirt paths
are replaced by streets paved with gold. Perhaps most wondrous
in that dry climate, the city boasts a river flowing through the
city, so that women need not trudge so far each morning to
fill up the family's water jugs. The American myth of the 19th
century lauded the freedom of the prairie and the possibilities
of homesteading, yet the diaries and correspondence of many
pioneer women record their dread in leaving their home city,
with its schools, churches, perhaps a library, friends, and
neighbors.

Sometimes Lent has been presented as a kind of retreat
from community. Individuals were to escape, at least mentally,

from the temptations of civilization, to focus on the private relationship between God and the self. However, the Lent unfolded in our Sunday Bible readings immerses believers back into the waters of baptism, and the baptismal font is crowded with the faithful of past, present, and future. The font is a city, not a prairie homestead with the nearest neighbors 160 acres away. Mary Magdalene met the risen Christ in a garden, but he sends her back to the city to meet with the assembled disciples.

Psalm 87 expresses the surprises of Lent: holy Zion includes even wicked Babylon; not only Israelites, but also Ethiopians were born in the city of God; and everyone joins the dance around its fresh water springs. Together we hope for this beneficent city.

> *Be the walls to protect us, O people-loving God. Be the wells from which we meet our need. Connect us with our neighbors, O Spirit of the Trinity. May it be so: Amen.*

Reading: Hebrews 11:8-16

Hymn: *ELW* 710, "Let Streams of Living Justice," stanzas 1, 3

THIRD SUNDAY IN LENT
GATHERING IN COMMUNITY

A
Exodus 17:1-7
Romans 5:1-11
John 4:5-42
Think about the many ways that we thirst.
Give thanks for rivers, rain, baptism.

B
Exodus 20:1-17
1 Corinthians 1:18-25
John 2:13-22
Think about each of the ten commandments.
Give thanks for the wisdom that comes from God.

C
Isaiah 55:1-9
1 Corinthians 10:1-13
Luke 13:1-9
Think about how distant we are from God.
Give thanks for Christ as a gardener.

Behold. Lord, an empty vessel that needs to be filled. My Lord,
fill it. I am weak in the faith; strengthen me. I am cold in love;
warm me and make me fervent, that my love may go out to
my neighbor. At times I doubt and am unable to trust you
altogether. O Lord, help me. In you I have sealed the treasure
of all I have. With me, there is an abundance of sin; in you
is the fullness of righteousness. Therefore I will remain with
you. Amen.
(A prayer of Martin Luther, *ELW* p. 87)

MONDAY OF LENT 3,
DAY SEVENTEEN
Water

*Jesus, tired out by his journey, was sitting by
the well.*
John 4:6, gospel for Lent 3 A

MANY OF US ARE accustomed to clean water being perpetually
available. We meet our need for water by merely walking to
one of our many faucets. But in Bible times and for many
people alive today, there is instead the communal well. The men
worked together to dig the well, and each morning the women
balance immense jugs on their shoulders to lug home the water
that the family needs for drinking, soaking the beans, washing
the body. When Abraham's servant met Rebekah at a well, she
watered his camels: how many jars of water were needed to
accomplish that chore? Jacob met Rachel, his future beloved, at
a well. Gideon and his troops camped by a well. The well is a
symbol of wholesome human community. We all need water; we
need one another's assistance to dig a well; we meet one another
daily at the well.

When there is no water, the people perish. The nomads were
dying of thirst, and the story says that when Moses struck the
rock, out gushed water so that all the people could drink. The
rabbis elaborated the legend, saying that the rock followed the
Israelites throughout their wanderings, so the people always
had access to water. Scholars suggest that one of the most
ancient passages in the Old Testament is the Song of the Well in
Numbers 21. "Spring up, O well!—Sing to it!—the well that the
leaders sank, that the nobles of the people dug." Delighted to
have water, the community sings its gratitude to the well.

We who have continual personal access to water might forget
that the water used at baptism was begun by God billions
of years ago, located in our terrain when the globe took its

present configuration, accessed by massive digging machines, collected in reservoirs somewhere in the neighborhood, and brought to the church by a system of pipes that other citizens manufactured. Here is the truth we learn by the baptism of infants: we are carried by others to the water that others have supplied. Even Jesus relies on the woman with her jar to quench his thirst. We might imagine the Trinity as a well: God the creator of water, God the water itself, God in the community that provides the water.

> *We need your ever-flowing grace, deep and refreshing God. Be our well of mercy. Provide our community the water it needs, and give us the jug with which to serve one another. May it be so: Amen.*

Reading: Genesis 21:14-20

Hymn: *ELW* 331, "As the Deer Runs to the River"

TUESDAY OF LENT 3,
DAY EIGHTEEN
Outsider

Just then [Jesus'] disciples came. They were
astonished that he was speaking with a woman.
John 4:27, gospel for Lent 3 A

MOST HUMANS ARE MOST comfortable when they are around
their own kind. People want to be inside a circle of others whose
color or religion or nationality or income or sexual style is like
their own, for the similarity makes them feel safe and normal.
Many people actually fear or even hate the outsider, seeing the
otherness as a threat. Genesis 26 tells of Isaac's servants who,
re-digging a well for use by their own people, encounter herders
who are outsiders. They shout, "The water is ours!" You're an
outsider: keep away from our water!

Religion asks of us to be something other than naturally
human. As Christians we attend to the story of Jesus and the
woman at the well. To a first-century pious Jewish man, she is a
three-time outsider: a Samaritan, a woman, and a law-breaker.
Yet Jesus drinks from her water-skin, for in Christ the outsider
is included. In the Gospel of Luke we hear of Jesus encountering
a four-time outsider: a Gentile demoniac who ran around naked
and lived among tombs. By the conclusion of the story, the man
is fully clothed and sitting peacefully at Jesus' feet, for in Christ
the outsider is included.

In many ways Jesus himself was an outsider. "Can anything
good come out of Nazareth?" asks Nathanael of a man who
broke Sabbath laws, dined with disreputable people, and was
executed by hanging on a tree. We who think of the cross as
sacred may be surprised by what is written in Deuteronomy
21 of anyone executed in this way: "Anyone hung on a tree is
under God's curse." Romans set up their crucifixions outside the
city walls, keeping the pollution of a dying criminal far away

from the community. To those who wished his execution, Jesus was recognized as outside the approved way of life, a threat to the status quo.

Keep the outsider outside, says the human community. Welcome the outsider, says baptism. When we see in faith that Christ is in the outsider, it may be easier to live in this Lenten, baptismal, counter-human way.

> *God beyond all we know, God inside the stranger,*
> *God executed outside the city walls, bring us to*
> *where you are. May it be so: Amen.*

Reading: James 2:1-8

Hymn: *ELW* 718, "In a Lowly Manger Born"

WEDNESDAY OF LENT 3,
DAY NINETEEN
Temple

Destroy this temple, and in three days I will raise it up.
John 2:19, gospel for Lent 3 B

IF YOU WANT TO know what an ancient Mediterranean temple
was like, look at the Lincoln Memorial in Washington, D.C.
On the summit of a hill or above a steep staircase is a pillared
pavilion housing a statue of the deity.

Temples are houses for the god or goddess, and a visit to the
temple is a way to honor the divine. In the ancient Near East,
monarchs constructed a temple adjacent to their palace, hoping
that the populace would see the regime as supported by the
gods. The biblical version of this is when King Solomon built
the first Jewish temple. Solomon's prayer at the dedication of the
temple admits that God does not actually live inside the temple.
What fills up the temple is the power of the name of God, and
to honor this name, the people are to come in pilgrimage at
festivals. Still today many pious Jews regard the ruins of the
temple (the Western or "Wailing" Wall) to be the place closest
to the ear of the Eternal One.

Christians have no temple. Throughout the centuries
Christians have assembled in homes, underground cemeteries,
public stadiums, classrooms, prisons, hospitals, on river banks,
under trees, and, yes, in consecrated specially-designed church
buildings. The place where Christians gather is not determined
by a statue of the deity or by some holy object that represents
and manifests divine power. Rather, Christians sit around a
Bible and a table, anywhere, everywhere. Of temples, Christians
have two things to say: Christ is the temple, and we are the
temple.

The Gospel of John says the first. We come closest to God
when we are embraced by Christ. Not a golden statue, Christ is

a person who touched the leper and ate meals with friends and strangers. Not a mythical hero, he was executed by the Roman criminal justice system. An odd temple! The letters of Paul say the second. As the body of Christ, we are now the temple. God lives in each of us and in the circle of us. Rather than presenting offerings to priests who maintain a sacred site, we get ourselves to worship on Sundays, and there hear and eat and drink God. A surprising temple!

Each week we sing the hymn that Isaiah heard when, visiting the temple, he saw in a vision the heavenly throne room of the Almighty. "Holy, holy, holy," we chant, joining the angels in their praise of God. Yet we are not having an ecstatic vision. We are in our little church, on a Sunday morning, helping one another through Lent, both celebrating now and always awaiting the resurrection. A Christian temple.

> *We cannot walk up all those steps, highest and almighty God. We have no statue befitting your majesty, Magnificent and Eternal One. Give us instead one another and some bread and wine. May it be so: Amen.*

Reading: 2 Corinthians 6:16—7:1

Hymn: *ELW* 652, "Built on a Rock," stanzas 1-3

THURSDAY OF LENT 3,
DAY TWENTY
Wisdom

God's foolishness is wiser than human wisdom, and
God's weakness is stronger than human strength.
1 Corinthians 1:25, second reading for Lent 3 B

ACCORDING TO THE CHINESE philosopher Confucius, wisdom
was the highest good. To learn wisdom, ask the old men for
advice. The elderly male authorities knew what mattered; others
need only attend to their instruction.

Chinese Daoists disagreed: Yes, wisdom was of the highest
value, but to discover truth, don't ask the old men; rather, take
a walk alongside a stream. The natural wisdom of the earth is to
be preferred over accumulated cultural knowledge.

Greek mythology also revered wisdom, personified as the
goddess Athena. Depicted fully armed, with the symbolic owl
on her shoulder, she had emerged by springing out of the head
of Zeus on a day that he had a migraine. So wisdom is like an
independent female, but she comes from the dominant male.

In the Bible are Jewish poems in which Wisdom is described
as a radiant primordial woman in the sky, the first creation
of God, who taught Israel religion and guided the people into
justice. Something like the chief justice of the Supreme Court,
Wisdom was a treasured aspect of the Eternal One, and her
teachings conveyed life to the people of Israel.

In many folk traditions, the old women are recognized as the
wells of wisdom. They bring infants to birth, heal the sick and
send the dead on their way. Among the Lenni Lenape of what is
now Pennsylvania, the old women chose the men who served as
tribal chiefs.

So which is the most reliable source of wisdom? Old male
rulers, or aged healing midwives? The ways of nature, or the
teachings of religion? Would our list include the innocent

child, or the Internet? Perhaps we despair that any trustworthy wisdom is available to befuddled humankind.

Christians call Christ our wisdom, our path through life, our insight concerning values, our understanding of justice. It is not that Christ hands out wisdom, a freebie on Sunday. Rather, we trust that Jesus is what we mean by "wisdom." The church must be wary if ever our proclamation of Christ sounds too similar to natural and normal wisdom. What assembles us each week is beyond human knowing, a wisdom somehow quite foolish.

We praise you for those who are wise, O God, our everlasting wisdom. Teach us the foolishness of your insight. Keep us on your crooked path to justice. May it be so: Amen.

Reading: Proverbs 8:1-12

Hymn: *ELW* 637, "Holy God, Holy and Glorious," stanzas 1, 2, 4

FRIDAY OF LENT 3,
DAY TWENTY-ONE
Harvest

*If it bears fruit next year, well and good; but if not,
you can cut it down.*
Luke 13:9, gospel for Lent 3 C

HARVEST, A RECENT BOOK describing a year on a Vermont
organic farm, makes it clear that, like the gardener in Luke's
parable, successful farmers cannot be sentimental about animals
and plants. If a lamb is born lame, it is killed and fed to the
pigs. If a vegetable sold poorly at last year's Saturday markets,
it was rooted out, so the soil can be more productive. If one
vegetable variety attracts too many pests, it must be replaced
by a more resistant strain. Harvesting as much good food as
possible requires a staggering amount of endless attention and
exhausting work.

Most of us do not grow our own food. Many of us are over a
century and a thousand miles from ancestors who did. Perhaps
we think of harvest only on Thanksgiving Day, with the dinner
table laden with a dozen different foods, without ever focusing
on the harvesting itself, everyone sharing the work of each.
During the last century, Midwestern farmers cooperated to
run the combine on one farm after another, and the all women
together cooked and baked the threshers' meals. Each farm
needed its neighbors.

The biblical story of Ruth deals with harvest. Naomi's dead
sons were named "sickness" and "consumption," and from
such starvation the two women escape to glean the fields, for the
Israelite God of justice had commanded harvesters to leave some
grain on the stalk, some lying in the rows, for the poor to gather
up and so eke out a meal. Rich Boaz, with his abundant harvest,
must attend to the starving peasants. The story concludes more
bountifully than many in human history: the harvest is shared,

Ruth gets her husband, Naomi her boy child, and Israel its king David.

Let Lent be a harvest in our lives. All that is not productive, out it goes, fed to the pigs, so there is space and energy for what will grow bountifully in the Spirit. It's laborious work, picking the bugs off the leaves. And let Lent be a harvest in our church, where we join the threshing crews, readying the community for Easter's baptisms, each week sharing the food of God. For Lent speaks the promise of the book of Ruth: food for the hungry, a home for the refugee, a king better than David who rises to give us life.

> O creator God, rainmaker, sun-sender, for food more than enough, we give you thanks; for companions with whom to work and eat, we give you thanks. For the starving of world, we plead: harvest us for them. May it be so: Amen.

Reading: Galatians 6:1-10

Hymn: *ELW* 508, "As Rain from the Clouds"

SATURDAY OF LENT 3, DAY TWENTY-TWO
Covenant

I will make with you an everlasting covenant, my steadfast, sure love for David.
Isaiah 55:3, first reading for Lent 3 C

WE OFTEN USE THE word *covenant* to describe a pledge between equals: I covenant with you to do something together. We like the idea of cooperation between comrades, two persons agreeing to work side by side.

But the biblical idea of covenant harkens back to ancient hierarchical society. The idea was that a master provided protection, food, status. In poetry of the Anglo-Saxons, the "loaf-ward"—English has shortened this word into "lord"— was also "giver of rings," supplying both necessities and rewards. In consequence, the vassals vowed loyalty and obedience, and they constituted his army. The arrangement was termed a covenant. In the Old Testament, we read of God's covenants with Noah, Abraham, the people of the exodus, and King David. God has saved in the past, continues to save, and promises to save in the future, and in response the people serve their lord. Something like a labor union's contract with the employer, the covenant binds together what is dissimilar, a people with their God.

In Christ we entered a covenant with God, and we need one another to meet our covenant obligations. Your godmother held you at baptism, and your pastor poured the water. Somebody prepares music for services, another brings treats for the coffee hour. We rely on the national church to help us probe moral issues and to send our contributions to refugee camps. Americans like to boast about the self, but Christians know that the self requires the assembly.

Lent is an annual exercise in covenant renewal. God has called us, baptized us, and set us within community. As our loaf-ward, God provides us food for life and hope. We respond by giving thanks, which is what the word "eucharist" means, and by serving that Lord with our lives. On Sunday we meet to remind one another of the particulars of this covenant: now, what is it that God has done? And what have we promised in return? Forty days of this conversation, and we will be ready for the public renewal of our baptismal vows at the great Vigil of Easter.

> *Covenant Lord, giver of life, keeper of promises,*
> *uphold us forever with your steadfast, sure love,*
> *and bind us once again to each other. May it be so:*
> *Amen.*

Reading: Joshua 24:1-7, 13-14, 16-18

Hymn: *ELW* 457, "Waterlife"

FOURTH SUNDAY IN LENT
RECEIVING MERCY

A
1 Samuel 16:1-13
Ephesians 5:8-14
John 9:1-41
Think about the ways that we live in darkness.
Give thanks for the light of Christ.

B
Numbers 21:4-9
Ephesians 2:1-10
John 3:14-21
Think about all our snake bites.
Give thanks for the promise of eternal life.

C
Joshua 5:9-12
2 Corinthians 5:16-21
Luke 15:1-3, 11b-32
Think about what in our lives needs to pass away.
Give thanks for the feast God provides.

Power of the eternal Father, help me. Wisdom of the Son,
enlighten the eye of my understanding. Tender mercy of the
Holy Spirit, unite my heart to yourself. Eternal God, restore
health to the sick and life to the dead. Give us a voice, your own
voice, to cry out to you for mercy for the world. You, light, give
us light. You, wisdom, give us wisdom. You, supreme strength,
strengthen us. Amen.
(A prayer of Catherine of Siena, *ELW* p. 87)

MONDAY OF LENT 4,
DAY TWENTY-THREE
Light

[Jesus said], "I am the light of the world." . . . Then
[the blind man] went and washed and came back
able to see.
John 9:5, 7, gospel for Lent 4 A

AT BEDTIME, THE TODDLER asks for a night-light because
humans rejoice in being able to see. Life as we know it requires
light, and so we ought not be surprised that many religions
speak of spiritual awakening as enlightenment. For even with
one's eyes open, one might see little that is important. During
the early centuries of the church, the story of Jesus giving sight
to the man born blind was used to describe baptism. Like the
man born blind, we too went and washed and came back able
to see.

So what can Christians see? In the dark of the year,
northerners gather on December 25 to celebrate that "the light
shines in the darkness, and the darkness did not overcome it."
On January 6, we come to Christ with the magi, for the light of
the world has come, and the glory of the Lord has risen upon
us. On Transfiguration, we glimpse Jesus dazzling bright as the
sun. At the Easter Vigil, God begins creation anew by filling the
universe with light. The Bible speaks of our hope for the end of
time, when there will be no more night, nor any need of lamp
or sun, for the Lord God will be our light. Sunday after Sunday
throughout the year, the Spirit of God shines a light on us, and
we are knocked off our horses to walk in the light of Christ.

What else can Christians see? There next to the font is the
paschal candle, lit to remind us of our own enlightenment. What
else? We gaze at one another and see the body of Christ, shining
in pew after pew. What else? No matter how dark is our world,
our family, or our own hearts, we can see by the light that a
merciful God provides.

The word *Lent* derives from the lengthening of the days in the early spring in the northern hemisphere. The night of the world is long, but as Easter approaches, the hours of daylight lengthen. By Easter itself, the hours of light are the same as the hours of darkness. So we are people of the light, illumining at least the space around us, sharing our lamp with our neighbors so they will not trip and fall.

> *In me is darkness; within the people is darkness; around us is darkness; at the end is darkness. Be our light, Radiant One, gleaming God, luminous Lord. May it be so: Amen.*

Reading: John 12:27-36

Hymn: *ELW* 306, "Come, Beloved of the Maker"

TUESDAY OF LENT 4,
DAY TWENTY-FOUR
Shepherd

He is keeping the sheep.
1 Samuel 16:11, first reading for Lent 4 A

"The Lord is my shepherd," begins the beloved psalm. With poems such as this, the Hebrew people pulled the transcendent God out of the distant beyond and into their own lives. We read the stories of the shepherds Abel, Rachel, Jacob, Moses, and Amos, and of wealthy men such as Abraham, Lot, and Job who owned vast flocks. Even King David was at first a shepherd. Sheep were God's gift to the people, the source of their livelihood, their food, their clothing, and their religious sacrifices. Without sheep the people could not live. Thus the people did not think of themselves apart from sheep: they were sheep, and their shepherd was God.

Perhaps because the poem of Psalm 23 is spoken by an "I," or perhaps because our church art depicts Christ carrying a single lost sheep, many Christians think of themselves as one lone lamb. However, the church fathers taught that Psalm 23 was not only the poem of an ancient herder, but is also the song for the Christian assembly as it approaches baptism at the Easter feast. The "green pastures" of verse 2 were seen as referring to the biblical instruction in the faith. The "still waters" is the baptismal font, where we receive the Holy Spirit, who "restores our soul." Baptism immerses us into the death of Christ, and it is this "valley of the shadow of death" through which we walk. But the resurrected Christ is with us in his word, "the rod and staff" of verse 4. The "table" is the bread and wine of holy communion, and the "oil" the anointing that was part of the baptismal blessing. "The house of the Lord" is our life within the body of Christ, both now and forever. The faithful were urged to pray Psalm 23 as Easter neared. The Vigil of Easter was the primary occasion for baptism, and even for those who had long since been baptized, Easter was the annual renewal of the entire community in baptism.

For us, then, Resurrection Day is not time travel, a memory event about what happened to Jesus long ago. Rather, it is the flock of sheep once again drinking at the river of life. It is the herd led by the staff of the shepherd to meadows of fresh grass. A wolf is always lurking, and nearby is a dangerous precipice, but thanks to the sacrifices of the shepherd, we are safe, huddling together for comfort and warmth. We are the flock grateful for such a caring shepherd.

> *Feed us, water us, guide us, O God our shepherd.*
> *Herd us into safety at night. May your crook be*
> *gentle around our necks. May it be so: Amen.*

Reading: Ezekiel 34:11-16

Hymn: *ELW* 780, "Shepherd Me, O God"

WEDNESDAY OF LENT 4,
DAY TWENTY-FIVE
Tree

Just as Moses lifted up the serpent in the wilderness,
so must the Son of Man be lifted up.
John 3:14, gospel for Lent 4 B

IN MANY CULTURES AND religions we encounter the image of the tree of life. Usually evergreen or magnificently leafed, the tree bears miraculous fruits or healing leaves, provides refuge for all the birds of the air, and connects earth and sky. Such a mythic tree stands in the center of the community—or the center of our imagination—to signify life at its fullest. Nowadays this tree is on countless logos: attracted by the image of a grand tree, we feel inclined to shop from that catalog or purchase that health insurance.

But the Lenten tree surprises us. In the book of Numbers we read an odd tale of the Israelites suffering from snakebite. They beg for healing, and Moses tells them to look in faith toward a tree, and they will have new life. But the tree they must gaze at is a pole on which is draped a bronze serpent. In the Gospel of John we read that Jesus on the cross is like that serpent on the pole. We are healed, not by grinding up the nutritious leaves and enjoying delectable fruits, but by looking in faith at a tree stripped of its branches, on which we see not miraculous food, but a dying God.

Christians through the ages have painted and sculpted and sung of this odd tree. Many medieval churches display a crucifix that sprouts green foliage and multicolored flowers. In a popular print of the nineteenth century, Christ is nailed to a tree on which are all the fruits of a virtuous Christian life: on the left, disreputable characters are being lured into hell, and on the right, a preacher in his black gown beckons the faithful to heaven. "Sing, My Tongue," a hymn written fourteen hundred years ago and still sung each Holy Week, calls the cross "the noblest tree: none in foliage, none in blossom, none in fruit your equal be." The dead tree is sprouting life for all.

This tree of life fits well into the oddness of Lent. That forty days of more care for the poor, more prayer, and less focus on our self will bring us deeper into life, this is not what we might have imagined. That our Sunday community of baptized folk is becoming more and more the body of Christ, this is a surprise. That on Easter Day the dead Christ will arise and send out his Spirit throughout the world, this is not what nature expects. Indeed, only because of the Spirit given us in baptism would any of us see in the cross of Christ a tree of our life together.

> *We circle around your cross, O Crucified One.*
> *May your broken body be for us healing leaves and*
> *nourishing fruits. Give us a nesting place in your*
> *branches. May it be so: Amen.*

Reading: Revelation 22:1-5

Hymn: *ELW* 342, "There in God's Garden"

THURSDAY OF LENT 4,
DAY TWENTY-SIX
Family

Your brother has come, and your father has killed
the fatted calf, because he has got him back safe and
sound.
Luke 15:27, gospel for Lent 4 C

RECENTLY THERE HAS BEEN lots of talk about biblical family
values. Let's see: from Abraham through Solomon, every man
had as many wives and concubines as he could afford; Judah
commended his daughter-in-law for having seduced him; Ezra
demanded that every Jewish man abandon any wife who was
not Israelite; Jesus, who was single, praised his followers as
more blessed than the mother who nursed him; Paul urged
Christians to live celibate so as to focus on the end time; the
household codes stipulate that wives and children are to obey
the man of the home; yet Luke wrote that in order to love
Christ, one must hate "father and mother, wife and children,
brothers and sisters": yes, his Greek word is "hate."

But there is another side to the scriptures. Jesus taught
his followers to call the Holy One of heaven and earth "our
Father." Once again we are faced with the plural: "our." We
join together in prayer, a family newborn in baptism. Whether
we come to hate our natural parents or not, we find ourselves
surrounded by sisters and brothers, by the dozens, by the
millions, sharing a weekly family meal provided by a parent
who is beyond any father, beyond any mother.

For some Christians, calling God Father is gift, surprising
mercy. For other Christians, calling God Mother is gift,
surprising mercy. For yet others, both images are mucked up
by personal memories that, like a millstone attached to the
metaphor, drown "father" and "mother" in the depths of the

sea. But at least there are the brothers and sisters, the family formed, not by nature or by choice, but by Easter.

In the beloved parable, the elder brother rejected his sibling. He got along fine with his dad, but not with his obnoxious kid brother. This sounds painfully familiar, it being easier to love the Father whom we have not seen than the sisters and brothers bothering us throughout the day. A prayer for Lent is that our Easter adoption into the family of faith can be gift, surprising mercy.

> *O God, be a father to us: name us your heirs. O God, be a mother to us: gather us into your arms. Form us into the family of Jesus our brother. May it be so: Amen.*

Reading: 1 John 2:7-14

Hymn: *ELW* 640, "Our Father, By Whose Name"

FRIDAY OF LENT 4,
DAY TWENTY-SEVEN
Creation

If anyone is in Christ, there is a new creation:
everything old has passed away; see, everything
has become new!
2 Corinthians 5:17, second reading for Lent 4 C

THE BIBLE INCLUDES A number of creation stories. Genesis 1
and Psalm 104 are poems about the creation of the universe;
Genesis 2–3 is a narrative about the creation of human life on
the family homestead; Job 38 suggests that God is the universe's
architect, designer, mason, construction company, zookeeper;
John 1 proclaims that the supreme light of creation is Christ;
Revelation dreams about a final re-creation of earth. Scholars
of myth consider also the flood story a creation story: once
more watery chaos engulfs all that is, and God creates a new
beginning for earth and a new start for humankind.

In traditional Christian theology, the doctrine of creation was
less about a process of the earth's development, and more about
the sovereignty of God. God is beyond the earth, yet responsible
for its life, from the beginning of time to its end, and every
single day along the way. Likewise, the doctrine of the new
creation is less about what my eternity will be like, and more
about the everlasting creativity of God. The daily news of pain
and sorrow notwithstanding, the Christian hope is that even
were the earth destroyed and humankind obliterated, the Spirit
of God can create anew. Baptism begins that new creation, one
believer at a time.

The church sets its annual calendar of celebration in such
a way as to tie together our observance of the life of Christ to
the very earth itself. On Christmas Day, the gospel reading is
the creation poem of John 1, so that Jesus' birth and the sun's
return coincide. At the Vigil of Easter, the first resurrection story

we read is Genesis 1, so that the universe itself is called into the newly created light. To connect Christ's resurrection with the annual re-creation of the northern hemisphere, Easter is always set on the first Sunday after the first full moon after the spring equinox. Because of the equinox, the daylight is equal to night, for we are halfway between winter and summer. Thanks to the full moon, even the night sky is bright. And Sunday, for Christians, is always the day of resurrection. Once again God is making a new creation, and Lent calls us to ready ourselves for whatever newness God has in mind.

Creator God, give life to the flowers and trees, to animals great and small. O Spirit of life, enliven our limbs and senses, our minds and emotions. Bring us together to the new life of your Easter. May it be so: Amen.

Reading: Isaiah 65:17-25

Hymn: *ELW* 407, "O Living Breath of God"

SATURDAY OF LENT 4, DAY TWENTY-EIGHT
Judge

In Christ God was reconciling the world to himself,
not counting their trespasses against them, and
entrusting the message of reconciliation to us.
2 Corinthians 5:19, second reading for Lent 4 C

WHEN THE APOSTLE PAUL wrote about forgiveness of our
trespasses, he was thinking about God as judge. According to
the Bible, God instructs the people in ethical life and also judges
sinful behavior, and this description of God, what Lutherans call
"law," filled the church's proclamation during medieval times.
In hundreds of European churches, sculpted over the main
doorway or painted in the front of the nave is Christ the judge,
welcoming those with beatific smiles into heaven and hurling
the terrified and twisted into hell. The Bible says that we need
to be reconciled with the divine judge who quite rightly has
condemned our actions.

These days many Christians hear mostly "gospel." God
is always ready to forgive, at least faithful worshipers. Even
though you are more or less party to the world's endless
injustices, not to worry! After all, God is perpetually smiling.

Lent calls us to focus more than we might on divine
judgment. The new heaven and earth promised in the coming
resurrection is a world of unnatural harmony: the lion and the
lamb nap side-by-side; those who were hungry will feast on free
food at mountaintop banquets. Whether, along with the trees of
Psalm 96, we will rejoice at the coming of the Judge depends on
which side of the world's injustices we have occupied. Will we
win or lose, when facing divine justice? Lent reminds us that to
rejoice in God's justice, we had better be, along with Mary, on
the side of the poor, the hungry, the homeless, the oppressed, the
war-torn, the unemployed—how long is the list?

Yet how can we stand alongside all those whose homes have been leveled by bombs? How can we spend nights with all the homeless in their cardboard shelters? It is a mercy that Lent is only forty days long, since attention to injustice is finally deep agony; for we cannot escape our own role in the cruelties of human society.

So each Sunday the body of Christ gathers once more to intercede for all who are in need. Our words put us in the shoes of all who cry out for justice, begging God that through the Spirit of the new creation there will be finally a feast for everyone.

> O God, mighty magistrate, everlasting judge, give justice to those at the bottom of every pile, and redistribute your bounty so everyone will have enough. Forgive us our sins, Merciful One. May it be so: Amen.

Reading: 1 Peter 1:13-25

Hymn: *ELW* 723, "Canticle of the Turning"

FIFTH SUNDAY IN LENT
AWAITING GOD'S PROMISES

A
Ezekiel 37:1-14
Romans 8:6-11
John 11:1-45
Think about how we are bones, how we will become bones.
Give thanks for Christ's call to life.

B
Jeremiah 31:31-34
Hebrews 5:5-10
John 12:20-33
Think about those seasons when we produce poor fruit.
Give thanks for the word of God in our hearts.

C
Isaiah 43:16-21
Philippians 3:4b-14
John 12:1-8
Think about all the rubbish in our lives.
Give thanks that God does a new thing.

Make us worthy, Lord, to serve our follow human beings
throughout the world who live and die in poverty and hunger.
Give them through our hands this day their daily bread, and by
our understanding love, give peace and joy, Amen.
(A prayer of Mother Teresa of Calcutta, *ELW* p. 87)

MONDAY OF LENT 5,
DAY TWENTY-NINE
Resurrection

Jesus said, . . . "I am the resurrection and the life."
John 11:25, gospel for Lent 5 A

EASTER PROMISES "RESURRECTION." THIS word is wide and
deep, a gleaming gift filled with many dreams and hopes. The
word packages up for us many stories about new life contained
in the Bible, and Lent invites us to reflect on all that resurrection
means.

"A grain of wheat falls into the earth and dies, and so bears
much fruit," is one description of resurrection. Well, we say,
the grain does not actually die: but it is buried in the earth,
down there with all the dust and ashes, and in what seems a
miracle it sprouts with new life, producing much more than it
first was, thirty-fold, sixty-fold, or a hundred-fold. The entire
earth is inundated by a flood, but Noah's family and the animals
reemerge from the ark to multiply yet more than all those who
had been destroyed. A boy, marked for sacrifice, is already tied
down on an altar, but at the last minute is saved by a ram. A
crowd of runaway slaves escapes the mighty army of the Pharaoh
of Egypt. Wisdom, described as a divine woman in the sky, calls
people away from the pathway to death and welcomes them to
a meal of bread and wine. There is a valley filled with dry bones,
and suddenly a leg bone begins to move, and then there are
skeletons coming together, and now full bodies are up on their
feet, and we see a renewed people praising God. A man trying to
run away from God gets thrown into the sea and swallowed by a
great fish that coughs him up three days later so he can, this time,
obey the word of the LORD. Three devout men get thrown into
a furnace of blazing fire, and even though the intense heat slays
the guards, the three faithful ones emerge as good as new, having
experienced a communion with a mysterious fourth.

This is what we are given: stories of the Spirit of God turning death into life, the Breath of the Almighty transforming chaos into a world of order and beauty. We are given also this: a community of faith, a rite of washing, and a weekly meal to strengthen our faith, to increase our love and hope. Always we are called further into the mystery of what "resurrection" means. In John 11, it is not Lazarus having a second life that is called resurrection. It is Christ who is the resurrection and the life. So this is what we are given: Jesus Christ.

Every day of our life we are dying, O God our creator. We beg for your resurrection, O God our savior. Give all who are gasping your sweet air, O God our breath. May it be so: Amen.

Reading: Colossians 2:20—3:4

Hymn: *ELW* 328, "Restore in Us, O God"

TUESDAY OF LENT 5,
DAY THIRTY
Clothing

*The dead man came out, his hands and feet bound
with strips of cloth, and his face wrapped in a cloth.
Jesus said to them, "Unbind him, and let him go."*
John 11:44, gospel for Lent 5 A

WHENEVER DOROTHY COULDN'T DECIDE what to wear in the
morning, her mother would quote her great-grandmother and
say, "If you don't know what to wear, you have too many
clothes." Probably the great-grandmother's house had no closets,
only several pegs by the bed. But some of us do have far too
many clothes: a jammed dresser, two closets full; don't throw
that tie away, it might be just the thing sometime next year, and
you never know when you might want those mauve high heels.

The vast majority of people alive do not mull over their attire
each day. Shall we imagine the clothing situation of much of
humankind? Their closet and dresser were washed away in the
flood. His monthly cash covers only food, with nothing left over
for shoes. She cannot schedule a job interview because she has
no appropriate clothes to wear. The family living in a refugee
camp has no place in the tent to store anything. Her clothes
were ripped off by the rapist. The rummage sale is stocked with
luxury dinner dresses, but has few men's trousers. You have
gained so much weight that none of your clothing fits.

In Lent we discover that we all need new clothes. We are
Lazarus in the tomb, wearing only strips of cloth. It is as if our
white baptismal robe has been torn into bandages, covering
up our dying face and binding our arms uselessly next to our
body. Or we are that first woman and first man, trying to cover
our nakedness with fig leaves. Or we are the runaway son,
ashamed of our rags, yet timid in the new robe and sandals. Or
we are the peculiar young man in Mark's passion account, who

escaping from Gethsemane leaves his linen cloak in the hands of the arresting officers and runs away stark naked.

We like to dress up for Easter Day, a flowered tie, a fancy hat. We look at one another, the community spiffed up in clean clothes, and smile. God's Spirit has clothed us, and all these colors are blending together into baptismal white. But we see white each Sunday in the vestment we call an alb, the robe of the baptized, the garb that announces our new birth.

Replace our dirty outfit with your white robe, O
God who dresses the earth and clothes the lilies. Be a
cloak to warm all who shiver in the night. May it be
so: Amen.

Reading: Luke 15:17-24

Hymn: ELW 648, "Beloved, God's Chosen"

WEDNESDAY OF LENT 5,
DAY THIRTY-ONE
Israel

These bones are the whole house of Israel. . . . Thus
says the Lord GOD: I am going to open your graves,
. . . and I will bring you back to the land of Israel.
Ezekiel 37:11, 12, first reading for Lent 5 A

SOME BIBLICAL IMAGES, SUCH as family and clothing, are
familiar to us, and easy to contemplate. Others are foreign and
their meaning for us elusive. A good example of the latter is the
biblical talk about Israel. When in our Sunday intercessions we
pray for Israel, we mean the contemporary State of Israel. But
when in the Sunday readings we hear of God speaking to Israel,
chastising Israel, promising life to Israel, and saving Israel, we
understand that God is addressing us. It is as if "Israel" is a
shorthand way to say "the people of God," and we have joined
with the Jews in claiming that title. Also we are Israel.

So when the Spirit of God blows life into Israel's dry bones,
we believe that the church is being enlivened by the resurrection.
When we join with Mary in her song, we are joined with the
Israel who is the servant of God. When in Advent we sing "O
come, O come, Emmanuel," we are the Israel to whom the
Savior is coming. When at the Easter Vigil we read the ancient
story of Israel crossing the sea, we think of our baptism, the
water through which we have been saved. When in a psalm God
calls Israel to faithfulness, we hear God beckoning us to the
moral life. When in the great prayer over the bread and wine we
thank God for saving Israel, we are praising the Eternal One for
leading us from death to life.

Like Israel of old, the church assembles to thank God for life.
Like Israel of old, we are called to live in a distinctive manner,
in relationship with God and in care for the earth and its
peoples. We are given simple food, our weekly bread and wine

like the manna from heaven. Supported by divine mercy, we are encouraged to see our life as already in the land of promise. Even when we feel ourselves to be only piles of dry bones, like ancient Israel we experience the Spirit's power. We stand up and live anew.

> *God of Abraham and Sarah, Miriam and Moses, David and Bathsheba, we beg you: be God for us. Embrace us, feed us, lead us, forgive us, restore our lives. May it be so: Amen.*

Reading: Ephesians 2:11-22

Hymn: *ELW* 250, "Blessed Be the God of Israel"

THURSDAY OF LENT 5,
DAY THIRTY-TWO
Spirit

You are not in the flesh; you are in the Spirit, since
the Spirit of God dwells in you.
Romans 8:9, second reading for Lent 5 A

WHEN WE HEAR THE word *spirit*, we might think of the
enthusiasm of the toddler; the positive attitude of a strong-
hearted victim; the eagerness of a returning student; the zeal
of the philanthropist; the lively feeling we get standing under a
springtime flowering tree; the communal loyalty to our school
or community or nation; the inner self of a loved one that we
hope will somehow live forever. Perhaps we think of those
energetic praise songs in a new worship book. The Bible speaks
of the divine spirit blowing life into the mud-man that God had
fashioned in Eden and the spirit of God resuscitating the valley
full of dry bones.

In all these references, "spirit" is positive, lively, even happy.
But Paul's letter to the Romans discusses Spirit in a paradoxical
way.

Part of what the church means by calling God Triune is that
God's Spirit is not wafting away up in the clouds, but resides
in the community of believers. We are, somehow, in God: that's
something to meditate on during Lent. If we are somehow
in God, our days will be marked not only by fulfillment
and joy. For there in God are all the poor, all the sorrows of
the human race, all the sufferings of Christ, even the entire
groaning creation. There in the Spirit of God will be not only
a magnificent magnolia, extravagant beauty enhancing our
church property, but also those cardboard lean-tos housing the
countless poor and the hospital emergency room with its terrible
news to parents.

The promise of Easter is that we are brought more and more into the Spirit of God, as that Spirit is entwined more and more with our being. At the Vigil of Easter, Christians remember their baptisms, perhaps marking themselves with a cross of water where the ashes had been. Yet in God's startling Spirit, the ashes are still there. The joy of divine presence and the sorrows of the suffering remain somehow together.

> *O God, you are breath of life, you are wind of springtime. O divine Spirit, come into us, and make room within us for all whom you bring. May it be so: Amen.*

Reading: Romans 8:12-27

Hymn: *ELW* 401, "Gracious Spirit, Heed Our Pleading"

FRIDAY OF LENT 5,
DAY THIRTY-THREE
Fish

Thus says the LORD, *who makes a way in the sea:*
. . ."I am about to do a new thing; . . . I will make
. . . rivers in the desert.
Isaiah 43:16, 19, first reading for Lent 5 C

IN THE STORY MOST beloved by the Jewish people, God saved
the Israelites from oppression by making a way in the sea for
them to escape on dry ground from Pharaoh's army. The torrent
they faced was no longer a barrier for them, no longer the
fearful abode of sea monsters, of fish huge enough to swallow
Jonah whole. Instead there was a pathway through the sea,
so they could complete their escape from the angel of death.
For centuries thereafter, the people sang Miriam's song of
gratefulness to God.

We Christians join in the song of our Jewish neighbors, for
Easter is our passage through the sea that we call baptism.
No more sea monsters can eat us up. Next week, on the night
that begins Easter, we who gather will also read of the Israelite
rescue through the sea, and perhaps dance to Miriam's song.

Just when we were relying on God to dry up the seas, God
does a new thing.

Isaiah's poem says that now God is making rivers in the
desert, flowing streams where there was only sand, waters
teeming with fish for everyone, so that Jesus can cook us a fish
breakfast when we arrive at the shore. We got accustomed to
the dry rocky ground called Lent, but we see before us a lake,
and there in the waters we glimpse a miraculous fish, and then
we remember that, if we were speaking Greek, the first letters of
the phrase "Jesus Christ, God's Son, Savior" spell "fish," and so
we enjoy a fish dinner in the desert, which is quite a new thing.
Perhaps this is what Christians were thinking when centuries

ago they traced a fish in the sand to say, "I am Christian," and their artists drew a fish on the platter in front of Jesus in their pictures of the Last Supper.

On Fridays in Lent, many Christians have eaten fish instead of meat. One explanation for this is that meat was served only to the wealthy, and so on Fridays, to remember the crucifixion, everyone ate the food of the poor. Perhaps, instead, Christians were readying themselves for the fish-fry with Jesus on the shores of the sea.

We pray to you, Jesus Christ, God's Son, Savior. Be food for all your people, and protect also the swarms of fish in your seas. May it be so: Amen.

Reading: Ezekiel 47:1-10

Hymn: *ELW* 817, "You Have Come Down to the Lakeshore"

SATURDAY OF LENT 5, DAY THIRTY-FOUR
Marriage

I was their husband, says the LORD.
Jeremiah 31:32, first reading for Lent 5 B

WHAT DOES IT MEAN to be married? Some young couples, writing their own wedding vows, promise each other an endless feeling of love. "I will love you forever and ever and ever," they say, and the old couples in the church listen wistfully. In the classic vows, the couple begins by promising faithfulness: "to have and to hold, for better for worse, for richer for poorer, in sickness and in health." Perhaps the feeling of love will continue, but surely it will wax and wane. Regardless, each vows to be there for the other. Dietrich Bonhoeffer said that it is not love that sustains the marriage, but marriage that sustains the love. Marriage is the commitment underneath the feeling.

Using the male imagery that was common at the time, the Bible speaks of God as a husband. Our God is wed, not to a goddess to produce more little deities, but to the people of Israel to bring forth justice and joy, and we Christians run up to the altar to get in on the promise. God vows to remain married to us, even as our love waxes and wanes. Easter promises that the Almighty One who is beyond all will hold us forever.

In England in the early 1400s lived a remarkable woman named Margery Kempe. She dictated her memoirs—the first in the English language—which you can buy at any good bookstore. After bearing fourteen children, she had a vision of Jesus telling her that now she was married to him. So she left her husband's bed and went off on one religious pilgrimage after another. She wore a wedding ring inscribed "Jesus is my love" that she said Christ told her wear, cried out in hysterics when at communion she took into herself the body of Christ, and criticized clergy for their meager devotion. Her memoirs make for lively reading.

Jeremiah means something else, however, than religious ecstasy. Not our wearing a mystical wedding ring, but God being faithful to all the people: no matter what, sickness, health, poverty, wealth, God will cherish us, just as God cherished also Jesus on both sides of the cross. And because God is holding on to us, we can hold onto God.

> *Loving God, embracing us in the night, we praise your faithfulness to your people. Marry us to your promises, and teach us commitment, one to another. May it be so: Amen.*

Reading: 1 Corinthians 13:1-13

Hymn: *ELW* 488, "Soul, Adorn Yourself with Gladness," stanzas 1, 2, 4

SUNDAY OF THE PASSION/PALM S
ENCOUNTERING CHRIST

A
Matthew 21:1-11
Isaiah 50:4-9a
Philippians 2:5-11
Matthew 26:14—27:66
Think about when we chose silver instead of God.
Give thanks for the fulfillment of God's promises.

B
Mark 11:1-11
Isaiah 50:4-9a
Philippians 2:5-11
Mark 14:1—15:47
Think about everyone who seems abandoned by God.
Give thanks for God's power, even when it is hidden.

C
Luke 19:28-40
Isaiah 50:4-9a
Philippians 2:5-11
Luke 22:14—23:56
Think about our lives as thieves.
Give thanks for the promise of paradise with God.

Lord, make us instruments of your peace. Where there is
hatred, let us sow love; where there is injury, pardon; where
there is discord, union; where there is doubt, faith; where there
is despair, hope; where there is darkness, light; where there
is sadness, joy. Grant that we may not so much seek to be
consoled as to console; to be understood as to understand; to
be loved as to love. For it is in giving that we receive; it is in
pardoning that we are pardoned; and it is in dying that we born
to eternal life. Amen.
(A prayer attributed to Francis of Assisi, *ELW* p. 87)

MONDAY IN HOLY WEEK,
DAY THIRTY-FIVE
Body

Mary took a pound of costly perfume made of pure
nard, anointed Jesus' feet, and wiped them with her
hair.
John 12:3, gospel for Monday of Holy Week

RECENTLY THERE HAS BEEN considerable interest in what
scholars call the Gnostic gospels, those many stories of the life
and meaning of Jesus that were written in the decades after the
biblical Matthew, Mark, Luke and John. In news broadcasts,
novels, and films we hear of secrets between Jesus and Mary
Magdalene, secrets between Jesus and Judas, hidden truths that
promise eternal life to those who are initiated into the mysteries.
According to the Gnostic worldview, the earth is too filled with
evil to have been created by a good God. The body is a trap
for the spirit. The religious goal for the spirit is to escape from
everything that bogs down the spiritual, but only a few people
will given the secret of how to ascend out of the prison of
darkness into divine light.

The biblical gospels have a quite different message. The Bible
proclaims that God created the world and called it very good.
God loved the people of flesh so much that God took on a body
and walked this earth. God cares for the bodilyness of creation
and saves this earth. God's face shines on us with grace and mercy,
and the good news of this divine love is offered to everyone.

The gospel appointed for Monday in Holy Week celebrates
the body that God created, joined, and saved. Jesus himself has
a real body, feet that can be anointed. Mary of Bethany has
hands that honor the body of her beloved master, and her hair is
used as a towel. Jesus praises Mary for revering the living body
that all too soon will meet its death, and our week moves from
sitting at table with Jesus to laying his corpse in a tomb.

Inspired by the Scriptures, the church uses the word "body" in several ways. Jesus is the human body of God; the bread with which God feeds us is the body of Christ; and the community that is fed is also the body of Christ. The words spoken to each communicant, "The body of Christ," refer both to the bread we receive and to us who gather at the table. In Christ the human body becomes something closer to what God intended at creation, and we move toward that body in thanksgiving.

Holy Week is a time to think about death: the death of Jesus, our own death. Each of us is a body, and these precious bodies will die, and at that end we will grieve. But the more that we realize ourselves as part of the body of Christ that is raised to life in God, the less we will worry about the end of our small part of the body that God created, joined, and saved.

We look on your face, O transcendent and immortal
God, and you touch us as we kneel at your feet.
Hold in your arms all who today will die. May it be
so: Amen.

Reading: John 1:1-18

Hymn: *ELW* 750, "Lord, Thee I Love with All My Heart"

TUESDAY IN HOLY WEEK, DAY THIRTY-SIX
Day of the LORD

*Truly I tell you, I will never again drink of the fruit
of the vine until that day when I drink it new in the
kingdom of God.*
Mark 14:25, gospel for Passion Sunday B

MONOTHEISTIC RELIGIONS SPECULATE ABOUT the beginning
of time, and they also debate what will happen at the end.
Will humanity stand before God? How will each of us fare?
The ancient Jews imagined the Day of the LORD as the joyous
coming of justice. Finally the poor would be fed and the
oppressed set free. The righteous would be rewarded for their
life of faithfulness, and the wicked granted their just deserts.
Christians also have believed that on the final day, perhaps in
the distant future, but perhaps tomorrow, divine judgment will
separate once and for all the good from the evil, heaven for the
sheep and hell for the goats. Some Christians seem a bit too
gleeful, thinking of all those miserable goats.

Mark's Gospel, the earliest written of the four in the Bible,
speaks another way about the coming day. At supper the night
before his death, Jesus vows not to drink wine again until the
day of the coming kingdom, and so we are surprised, as we read
on in Mark, that Jesus does drink wine again, just before he
dies.

There is nothing more natural than the hope that eventually
the good guys will get rewarded and the bad guys will get sent
into outer darkness. Yet Mark's account challenges our usual
expectations. On the day we call Good Friday, Jesus is executed
with criminals. It becomes dark at noonday. A centurion in the
army that was responsible for carrying out the death sentence
acclaims Jesus as the Son of God. What we thought was good
and what we assumed was bad are turned around. The gospel

writer proclaims that on the day of Christ's crucifixion, the world as we know it did come to its end. When we gather each week to remember this death, we join with Jesus in sharing the wine of the kingdom, strangely already arrived by faith. The death of Christ has brought into time a new day, and that day goes on and on.

We are offered a community of faith, living each day, propelled out of the day, toward the day. We abide in the hope that beyond retribution is mercy; beyond just deserts is a surprising God.

> *Give to us, most merciful God, the new day of the death and resurrection of your Son. Perfect our justice with your mercy. May it be so: Amen.*

Reading: Isaiah 25:6-9

Hymn: *ELW* 726, "Light Dawns on a Weary World"

WEDNESDAY IN HOLY WEEK, DAY THIRTY-SEVEN
Kingdom

Jesus, remember me when you come into your kingdom.
Luke 23:42, gospel for Passion Sunday C

"ONCE UPON A TIME, there was a king." The countless fairy tales that begin with these words play upon the myth of kingship: that at the head of the social order is a good and brave man, wise and just, who oversees his country so that the people thrive, safe and contented. He belongs up there on top: perhaps God put him there. The people are well served, living in peace with their neighbors and in harmony with one another.

But then we hear the whole of the fairy tale, and we encounter the troubled truth wrapped inside the gorgeous packaging. As the prophet Samuel warned the Israelites when they desired a monarch, the king will commandeer your sons to serve in his army; he will take your daughters to spruce up his palace; he will convert your farmlands into gardens for his cronies; he will demand a tenth of your livelihood in taxes. Yet still the people wanted a monarchy. And so they got kings: David was guilty of adultery and murder, and Solomon, lauded as the wisest man in the world, had three hundred wives and seven hundred concubines. Kings are definitely a mixed bag.

But, despite the power grabs, brutal wars, and high taxation commonplace with monarchs, the myth of the king offers much that is good: a stable social order; strict laws and effective justice; secure borders; decent roads; clean hospitals; famine relief. Many who live without a monarch still hold in their imagination the archetypal image of the magnificent sovereign. And so we visit the palaces of Queen Elizabeth or read historical novels about famous kings and their adventures.

In describing God, the Bible uses the metaphor of monarchy more than any other. God is the one who rightly stands at the head, administering justice, providing food for the poor, protecting the vulnerable. In this way, the Bible is like other religious writings, describing the deity like a king or queen. But in Holy Week we say a more disquieting prayer. We name Jesus our king. Yet, with such a crown, such a throne, streaks of blood instead of rows of rubies, this king turns our expectations upside down. Only by breathing the new life of the Spirit can we praise this man as king.

Shape our hopes by your Spirit, O God, mighty sovereign. Make us desire what you promise, benevolent ruler. Anoint us for service in your kingdom. May it be so: Amen.

Reading: Acts 17:1-9

Hymn: *ELW* 431, "O Christ, What Can It Mean for Us"

MAUNDY THURSDAY,
DAY THIRTY-EIGHT
Servant

Jesus . . . tied a towel around himself. Then he
poured water into a basin and began to wash the
disciples' feet and to wipe them with the towel that
was tied around him.
John 13:4-5, gospel for Maundy Thursday

FOR THE WORD *SERVILE*, our dictionaries give as synonyms
"bootlicking, submissive, abject, obsequious, menial, base." No
one wants to be servile.

About the word "server": in restaurants all over the United
States nowadays, the server introduces herself—"Hi, I'm Susie, and
I'll be your server"—and proceeds with broad smiles to announce
the specials and list their ingredients. This ritual suggests that she
is a personal friend. We know her by her first name. She is on the
same level as the customer, glad to chat with us.

At a university, "service projects" include volunteering to
build a community center in Appalachia. The week involves
plenty of work, but is also a splendid bonding experience with
your college friends. You'll never forget the fun you had.

All this is alien to the worldview of the Bible, which assumed
that humankind is layered into rigid classes and that servants
are essential to the well-being of the society. Even Paul sends the
runaway slave Onesimus back to his owner.

On Maundy Thursday Jesus is the servant, down on his
knees, performing menial tasks for his company. More churches
each year are reviving this ritual, each person getting washed
and then washing the next. Here at the end of Lent we enact the
body of Christ: Jesus created us into a community of servants,
and each of us both gives service and receives the service of
others.

Some of us are good at serving others, bringing a casserole
to the church supper, running errands for shut-ins, writing large
checks for famine relief. Some of us are used to being served:
we gladly pay a small amount of money to someone else who
will wash our clothes, clean our home, shovel snow off our
driveway. But on Maundy Thursday the servants and the served
can no longer be so clearly separated out, by economic reality or
personality inclination. We are all both, one body, your feet, my
feet.

> *O God, divine majesty, we see you kneeling before*
> *your servants. Train our knees to bend before one*
> *another. Make us gracious in receiving the service of*
> *others. May it be so: Amen.*

Reading: Galatians 5:13-25

Hymn: *ELW* 358, "Great God, Your Love Has Called Us"

GOOD FRIDAY, DAY THIRTY-NINE
Emanation of the divine

Then [Jesus] bowed his head and gave up his spirit.
John 19:30, gospel for Good Friday

SOME POPULAR BIBLE TRANSLATIONS render this passage, "Jesus bowed his head and died." But other translations, like the one cited above, attempt to retain as much as possible of the original Greek, which literally says "he handed over the spirit." These translators maintain that the evangelist is saying two things: Jesus died, and something has happened in the world through that death.

Some scholars describe religion as the perennial human endeavor to achieve what is divine, each religion offering its own answer to the question of how to access a life more ultimate than our own. The Gospel of John names God as the creator of life, the source of light, the origin of word. All that we humans count as good begins in God and comes (emanates) from God. Greek philosophers would have been familiar with the idea that life flows out from God. However, to this notion of "divine emanation" the evangelist adds the religious faith of the Jewish people: God is not only mind, abstract power, but also heart, ultimate love. God radiates not only thought, but also mercy.

We Christians encounter this God best in the life of Jesus. Christ comes from God, like water from the fountainhead, like light from the sun. Christ emerges from the truth that is God, and he is the way for us to enter into that truth. In Christ we encounter abstract power and ultimate love.

John writes that at his death, Jesus sent his Spirit out to us. By that Spirit, we become connected to the Triune God. Through that Spirit, we receive the gifts God offers. In that Spirit, we are transformed into a conduit of divine grace for all the world.

We come to understand why the church calls this Friday Good. We trust in God as the source of life, mercy, grace, joy, comfort; all this comes to the world through the life and death of Christ. The divine compassion that Christ embodied is available also to us, and through us to others. St. Augustine called the Trinity the lover, the beloved, and love. We who are baptized are now in this chain of love, this transfer of mercy, this river of life. When Jesus cried out, "It is finished," his work was completed, but through his Spirit, ours continues.

O God, you are the endless source of blessing;
for centuries your mercy reaches us from the cross.
Connect us to yourself and with all who cry out
for your blessing. May it be so: Amen.

Reading: John 14:1-14

Hymn: *ELW* 602, "Your Heart, O God, Is Grieved"

HOLY SATURDAY, DAY FORTY
Battle

Pilate said to them, "You have a guard of soldiers;
go, make [the tomb] as secure as you can "
Matthew 27:65, gospel for Holy Saturday

ALTHOUGH MOST CHURCHES DO not have a service on Holy
Saturday until the great Vigil of Easter after sundown, Bible
readings are appointed for this interim day. The gospel is the
story from Matthew about Pilate agreeing to post sentries at
Jesus' tomb. It seems that even after Jesus' death, the power
struggle continued. Soldiers are stationed at Jesus' grave, the
Roman guards standing ready with shields and spears to fight
against the enemy. One might imagine that with the leader of
the religious sect dead and his followers in hiding, the battle
would be over, but Matthew writes that in the minds of Jesus'
opponents, the war goes on.

Christians agree that the conflict between good and evil
continues, from the beginning of human time, through Good
Friday and until our end. Rousing hymns describe the battles
that the faithful must fight. People who suggest that evil is small,
vulnerable, not a serious problem, easily overcome, are denying
a central Christian conviction, that evil is massive, powerful, a
perpetual enemy of our God that continues to plague the world.

Early theologians described the crucifixion as a battle that
the devil thought he had won, only to discover on Easter Day
that Christ has conquered evil. Children know this idea from
the war between Aslan and the White Witch in stories by C.S.
Lewis. The Book of Revelation describes such a war at the
beginning of time. Lucifer, the angel bearing God's light, tried to
take over heaven. The archangel Michael and the good angels
fought against Lucifer and the evil angels, and Michael threw
Lucifer down into hell. It's the story of the Garden of Eden writ
large: creatures who strive to become God are expelled from the

presence of the Almighty, but the conflict is so momentous that we imagine it as a war.

We know this battle, not only between massive human forces, such as Nazis versus the Allies, but also within our hearts. For forty days we have faced this evil, relied on the power of our baptism to thwart it, united with the community against it, praised God for supporting us in spite of it, and lived for a future marked not by this evil, but by divine promise. And next year we will come to another forty days and forty nights, for the fight goes on.

But tomorrow is the celebration of the victory.

Victorious God, triumphant champion, be our shield on the field of battle, and protect us until the armistice that only you can bring. May it be so: Amen.

Reading: Ephesians 6:10-18

Hymn: *ELW* 805, "Lead On, O King Eternal!"

FIFTY DAYS OF EASTER

Here are some hymns to sing during the fifty days of Easter that recall many of the images from your forty days and forty nights:

ELW 377, "Alleluia! Jesus Is Risen!"
ELW 383, "Christ Is Risen! Shout Hosanna!"
ELW 308, "O Morning Star, How Fair and Bright!"
ELW 793, "Be Thou My Vision"
ELW 826, "Thine the Amen, Thine the Praise"